COLLECTABLES

Guitars

This is a STAR FIRE book

STAR FIRE BOOKS
Crabtree Hall, Crabtree Lane,
Fulham, London SW6 6TY
United Kingdom

www.star-fire.co.uk

First published 2008

08 10 12 11 09

1 3 5 7 9 10 8 6 4 2

Star Fire is part of The Foundry Creative Media Company Limited

© The Foundry 2008

The CIP record for this book is available from the British Library.

ISBN: 978 1 84786 206 8

Printed in China

Thanks to: Chelsea Edwards and Nick Wells

Picture Credits
Images courtesy of: DK Images: page 7, 9, 13, 15, 17, 23, 25, 27, 29, 31, 33,
39, 41, 45, 47, 51, 57, 59, 61, 63, 65, 67, 69, 71, 72; Gibson Guitars: 21, 37;
Hauser Guitars: 11; Parker Guitars: 49; Paul Reed Smith Guitars: 53, 55;
Private Collection/Foundry Arts: 19; Shutterstock: 1, 3, 4, 35, 37, 43

COLLECTABLES

Guitars

Jake Jackson

STAR FIRE

Foreword

You don't have to play the guitar to love it – the shape, the tone, the sheer sexiness of it. From the early classicals, through the amazing jazz archtops to today's wierd and wacky electric variations, the guitar has taken a grip on popular imagination and its ubiquity reflects the accelerated impact of music and its icons on our daily lives. Whether you're into country or flamenco, hard electric rock or jazz fusion, this litle book is the one for you.

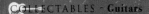

Gibson SJ-200

Body style: acoustic flat top

Country of origin: USA

Date of manufacture: 1938

Primary music style: country

Played by: Gene Autrey,

Beth Orton,

Ray Whitley

Selmer-Maccaferri

Body style:	**acoustic flat top**
Country of origin:	**Italy**
Date of manufacture:	**1955**
Primary music style:	**jazz**
Played by:	**Django Reinhardt, Steve Hackett**

Santos Hernández

Body style:	flamenco
Country of origin:	USA
Date of manufacture:	*c.* 1918
Primary music style:	jazz
Played by:	Ramon Montoya, Niño Ricardo

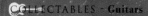
Stromberg Master 400

Body style:	archtop
Country of origin:	USA
Date of manufacture:	*c.* 1938
Primary music style:	jazz
Played by:	Freddie Green, Fred Guy

D'Angelico New Yorker

Body style:	**archtop**
Country of origin:	**USA**
Date of manufacture:	**1937**
Primary music style:	**jazz**
Played by:	**Perry Bechtel,**
	Pete Townshend

D'Aquisto New Yorker

Body style:	archtop
Country of origin:	USA
Date of manufacture:	*c.* 1967
Primary music style:	jazz
Played by:	Larry Coryell, Joe Pass

National Style O

Body style:	resonator
Country of origin:	USA
Date of manufacture:	1935
Primary music style:	blues
Played by:	Son House, Mark Knopfler

Gibson ES350

Body style:	semi-acoustic
Country of origin:	USA
Date of manufacture:	1947
Primary music style:	jazz
Played by:	Tal Farlow, Barney Kessel

Gretsch 6120 Chet Atkins Hollow Body

Body style:	semi-acoustic
Country of origin:	USA
Date of manufacture:	1955
Primary music style:	jazz
Played by:	Chet Atkins,
	Eddie Cochran,
	Duane Eddy

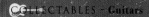

Gretsch 6120
Country Gentleman

Body style: semi-acoustic

Country of origin: USA

Date of manufacture: 1957

Primary music style: jazz

Played by: Chet Atkins,

George Harrison

Rickenbacker 360-12

Body style:	**semi-acoustic 12 string**
Country of origin:	**USA**
Date of manufacture:	**1964**
Primary music style:	**rock**
Played by:	**Chris Martin,**
	Roger McGuinn,
	Tom Petty

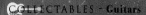

Ovation Balladeer

Body style: electro-acoustic

Country of origin: USA

Date of manufacture: *c.* 1966

Primary music style: jazz, rock

Played by: Joan Armatrading,

                               Glen Campbell

Takamine TNV 460SC

Body style: electro-acoustic

Country of origin: Japan

Date of manufacture: 1955

Primary music style: country, folk

Played by: John Scofield,
                             Bruce Springsteen

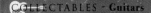

Gibson Les Paul Goldtop

Body style: solid body electric

Country of origin: USA

Date of manufacture: 1952

Primary music style: rock, rock'n'roll

Played by: Duane Allman,
Brian Jones

Gibson Les Paul Classic

Body style:	**solid body elecric**
Country of origin:	**USA**
Date of manufacture:	**1960/1990 (reissue)**
Primary music style:	**rock**
Played by:	**Buck Dharma,**
	Pete Townshend

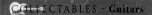

Gibson Les Paul Custom

Body style:	**solid body electric**
Country of origin:	**USA**
Date of manufacture:	**1957/2007 (reissue)**
Primary music style:	**rock**
Played by:	**Mark Bolan,**
	Jimmy Page

Gibson Explorer

Body style:	solid body electric
Country of origin:	USA
Date of manufacture:	1958
Primary music style:	rock
Played by:	The Edge, Dave Grohl

Gibson SG

Body style:	solid body electric
Country of origin:	USA
Date of manufacture:	1961
Primary music style:	pop, rock
Played by:	Jimi Hendrix, Tony Iommi

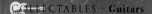

Gibson Flying V

Body style:	solid body electric
Country of origin:	USA
Date of manufacture:	1958
Primary music style:	blues, rock
Played by:	Dave Davies, Albert King

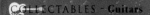

Fender Telecaster

Body style:	solid body electric
Country of origin:	USA
Date of manufacture:	1969
Primary music style:	pop, rock
Played by:	Jonny Greenwood,
	Bruce Springsteen

44

Fender Stratocaster

Body style: solid body electric

Country of origin: USA

Date of manufacture: 1954

Primary music style: pop, rock

Played by: Jeff Beck,

                             Dave Gilmour

Parker Fly

Body style:	solid body electric
Country of origin:	USA
Date of manufacture:	1992
Primary music style:	jazz, rock
Played by:	The Edge,
	Joni Mitchell,
	Keith Richards

Burns Bison

Body style:	**solid body electric**
Country of origin:	**UK**
Date of manufacture:	*c.* **1962**
Primary music style:	**pop, rock**
Played by:	**Elvis Presley,**
	Bruce Welsh

PRS Standard 24

Body style:	solid body electric
Country of origin:	USA
Date of manufacture:	1955
Primary music style:	latin, rock
Played by:	Ted Nugent, Carlos Santana

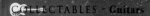

PRS Singlecut

Body style: solid body electric

Country of origin: USA

Date of manufacture: 1995

Primary music style: rock

Played by: Andrew Latimer,

Mike Smith

Gretsch 6129 Silver Jet

Body style:	**solid body electric**
Country of origin:	**USA**
Date of manufacture:	**1955**
Primary music style:	**rock'n'roll**
Played by:	**Billy Zoom**

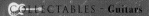

Framus Nashville

Body style:	solid body electric
Country of origin:	Germany
Date of manufacture:	1975
Primary music style:	blues, jazz
Played by:	Peter Green,
	Dan Lamb

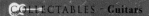

Aria Urchin Deluxe

Body style: solid body electric

Country of origin: Japan

Date of manufacture: 1977

Primary music style: rock

Played by: metal heads

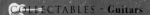

Yamaha SG2000

Body style:	solid body electric
Country of origin:	Japan
Date of manufacture:	1976
Primary music style:	rock
Played by:	Jake Burns,
	Frank Zappa

Yamaha Pacifica

Body style:	solid body electric
Country of origin:	Japan
Date of manufacture:	1955
Primary music style:	pop, rock
Played by:	Michael Lee Firkins, Mike Stern

Gibson EBSF-1250 Double Neck

Body style:	twin-neck electirc
Country of origin:	USA
Date of manufacture:	1962
Primary music style:	rock
Played by:	Mike Rutherford, John Wetton

Hofner 500/1 Violin Bass

Body style: bass electric

Country of origin: Germany

Date of manufacture: 1961

Primary music style: pop, rock

Played by: Paul McCartney

Steinberger Headless Bass

Body style:	solid body electric
Country of origin:	USA
Date of manufacture:	1979
Primary music style:	jazz fusion, rock
Played by:	Lemmy Kilmister, Mike Rutherford